Crossing the Salt Flats

By the Same Author

Crossing the Salt Flats

✪

Christopher Wiseman

The Porcupine's Quill

CANADIAN CATALOGUING IN PUBLICATION DATA

Wiseman, Christopher
Crossing the salt flats

Poems
ISBN 0-88984-210-8

I. Title.

PS8595.I8C66 1999   C813'.54   C99-932541-8
PR9199.3.W57C66 1999

Published by The Porcupine's Quill,
68 Main Street, Erin, Ontario NOB 1TO.
Readied for the press by John Metcalf; copy edited by Doris Cowan.
Typeset in Ehrhardt, printed on Zephyr Antique laid,
and bound at The Porcupine's Quill Inc.

The cover image is after a photograph of the Salt Lake Desert, Utah.

Represented in Canada by the Literary Press Group.
Trade orders are available from General Distribution Services.

We acknowledge the support of the Ontario Arts Council,
and the Canada Council for the Arts for our publishing program.
The financial support of the Government of Canada
through the Book Publishing Industry Development Program
is also gratefully acknowledged.

I   2   3   ·   OI   OO   99

Canada

For Jean

with me all the way on the salt flats

Polished maroon and gold, chrome dazzling,
my proudest possession as a teenager,
it was a bike envied by friends, looked at
by strangers, kept immaculate by cloths
soft as clouds. Every spoke was cleaned.
I kept it locked at school, let nobody ride it.
It was a deep pure passion.

I see you in your school uniform
waiting for me in the shop doorway.
I rode the bike, whirring, shining, racing
from my school to yours. I could do it
in four minutes, standing on the pedals
strong and manly, but more than that
made my pulse hammer when I saw you there.

Back again today. I had to see.
Forty years on, and I walk around.
Part of your school is now the Queen of Hearts
Restaurant, with an outdoor patio
by the main road, near where you waited,
full of loud ones eating and laughing.
Part is Scruffy Murphy's Irish Pub.
Sacrilege. But the doorway's still here
where I used to stop that gleaming bike
in a skid, leap off it, leg over handlebars,
see your smile. White blouse, brown
uniform. Mine was dark blue and grey.

Our walks together, you and I, under trees,
around the hard mud lanes, some still here,
together, together, away from roads and people,
my blood singing, one arm round you, one on the bike.
What more could I have asked at fifteen?

Queen of Hearts. We could sit here today,
I think, dressed casually, colourfully,
on the patio, toast our time and what we were,
sip wine, explore our lives. It would be fine, fine
to know you now, to drive you in a shining car!
Our special song was 'My Resistance Is Low'.

How we'd walk from there and hide ourselves!
You taught me how to kiss, how to touch
a hot bare breast. Right where I'm walking now.
I move on. That demure brown cloth,
the astonishing softnesses beneath it,
and how, turning to you, I didn't even hear
my bike crash down in the dirt, handlebars
twisted, front wheel spinning and spinning
as if it would turn my whole life.

ON JULIA'S CLOTHES
(A story from 1950)

We were some kind of cousins, you and I,
Though you were younger and your brother was
My friend. You tagged along when we went playing
In the woods or by the lake near your village.
I was around thirteen, come with my mother
To visit this less-known side of the family.
We didn't want to take you with us, got
Annoyed waiting for you to catch us up,
Said cruel things. But you wouldn't leave us.
Two visits. That's all. Julia. I forgot you.

Seems you had some problems, went to see
A shrink, fell hard for him. When he refused you,
Got impatient, sent you away, whatever,
You put your father's shotgun in your mouth.
Your mother found you, her quiet and only daughter.
Saw the walls and ceiling. Saw your clothes.

Just early twenties, and they say you were
Very bright, attractive, not strange at all.

I think of you trailing after us, a silent
Skinny ten-year-old. I remember how
The heavy berries hung in the long hedges,
The lake was a clear deep mirror, and we
Thought you were a nuisance and ignored you,
Little cousin, now quite far removed.

The cat had kittens at least three times a year.
We kept one for her milk, then gave it away.
My father killed the others. With some fear
I watched him once. First he took a spade
And dug quickly in the wet black soil
Behind the house, between the clumps of flowers.
Then a cloth bag. He filled the scrubbing pail
With cold tap water. Ignoring all the purrs
He took the three or four that were condemned,
Pulled them from their suckling without a word,
Carried them, blind fur slugs, in one hand
Outside. Face set. Softly they cheeped and stirred
As he dropped them roughly in the bag, spun
It closed, squatted, and with a sigh or cough
Pushed it deep into the water. Said none
Of the things I thought he might, just looked off,
Looked away from the bucket. No sound. No hurry.
Seemed like five minutes before he slopped it out
And shook them down into the hole. 'Bury
Them. Empty the pail,' he said, and left. It hurt.

Of all the ghosts who peopled my young life
Why do I ask you back? Ignorable
Then, at the monthly church dances, off
In a corner of the hall, no sound-system,
Your thin grey hair brilliantined shiny,
Just you and your dull, dented, silver sax
Playing melody in front of bass
And drums. Strict-tempo men from before the war,
Monotonously tight your ballroom rhythms,
The quicksteps, foxtrots, waltzes and valetas,
With no vocals or modern licks, though you
Sometimes tried current top-twenty tunes,

Sucking the life from them. The hokey-cokey
And the conga were your idea of cutting loose,
Though we – fourteen, fifteen – paid you no mind
In the hot throbbing of our fevered blood,
Our joys and humiliations. Standing in front
Of your rhythm men, you never looked at us

Or tapped a foot. Your eyes stayed fixed above
The dancing swirl of kids. Where were you then
As your sax played on and on all through
Those years of my young life? I'd know it now,
Playing our parents' tunes, the ones you knew –
'Harvest Moon', 'Always', 'What'll I Do?'

Nobody introduced you, you had no name –
You or the band. You were anonymous.
Came in two small cars, parked on the street,
And I think you were retired, playing church halls
For beer money, an envelope from the vicar.
Ignorable, I said. So why ask you
Back? Sometimes I watched you packing up,
Lighting smokes, putting on your raincoats,
Carrying the instruments to the cars,
Job done but hardly speaking, though I can't be sure,
Recalling all the dramas playing round me.

Why ask you back, now that the years have faded
You to shadows, the way all those become
Who help to make things happen, promise nothing,
Don't intrude? Because I can see your face
Up there as you played – it's never left me.
Because life's never been like that again,
So urgent, so important, with that steady
And steadying beat. Because, as I look back
To the little hall with its streamers and balloons,
I dance the last waltz again, ah, lights dimmed,
Hands on a waist, mouth in perfumed hair,
The unbearable soft push of silky hips,
Your sax struggling with 'My Heart Cries for You'.

Those two! How they sailed through my growing up!
Fur coats, cloche hats, much powder on their faces,
Oh they were stately ones as they passed in review,

Arm in arm. Out of place there. Their accents
Were from somewhere far away, somewhere
High and refined where everything was better,

Somewhere they'd come down from to our world.
Miss Nan McCardle. Miss Lucy Anderson.
Why, in their fifties, were they living there

Between us and the Shaws, opposite old Fanny?
No man crossed their threshold all those years,
But we didn't, in those days and with those two,

Consider things we might consider now.
We thought that one of them must have lost a husband,
Or a fortune. There'd been a tragedy, a fall,

We were sure. So long, so long they were next door,
The house dark and private next to our garden,
Their slow, full-sailed navigation of our streets.

We tried to avoid them, for their loftiness
Demanded deference from us, yet they ignored
Polite greetings if they were talking together,

Or rather whispering. They quietened the whole end
Of Scarisbrick Road just by being there.
Not women, ladies. Not ladies. More than that.

One taught music at a girls' high school.
The other stayed home, walked silently to the shops.
Why no pre-war Daimler or Lea-Francis

At their gate, high, black, with leather seats?
Why no house out in the leafier suburbs
With maid and gardener? It must have been money.

So quiet those two. But listen. From their house
Some evenings glorious full-blooded piano,
A vast passion washing over the city!

(Then my music lessons. A brass knocker.
Lucy grave at the door. That freezing front room.
Plump grey chairs, dust in the air, flower pictures,

The piano with a gilded metronome.
Always five minutes before Nan's sweeping entrance.
She made me learn the words and sing out loud

As I mangled simple songs from an old book.
Marjorie's on Starlight, I'm on Jack.
Isn't he a beauty, dear old Jack?

Marjorie are you ready? Wait till Jack
Is steady. Race you to the orchard there
And back. I've won! I wish I could forget it,

Forget the embarrassment, as full of pop songs,
Girls and football, I croaked out all that drivel.
Fear of her, that house, I suppose that's why

It's stuck. However hard I tried, I failed,
And she told me I was letting my parents down,
And I'd never – her horror! – manage 'The Blue Danube',

Never mind 'The Tritsch-Tratsch Polka'. I stopped
After a couple of months, but even today
I can hear that withering scorn and the metronome

Ticking the long minutes so slowly away,
Feel the clumsiness of my fingers, hate
Those rich little bastards with their ponies and orchard.

After that it was back to 'Good afternoon',
Though even frostier than before.) Those two
And their strange voyage through my youth. Long gone

Now, and gone oh gently, stylishly,
Gone differently from others, gone as if
In waltz time to the clicking golden hand,

Gone, waving together, the warm sudden notes
Of the upright, passionate on summer evenings,
Fading like the flowers in their pictures,

The dust slow-dancing in a shaft of sun.
They were not of our world, no, not heavy enough,
Not ordinary. Gone now, those curious ladies

And all their sad, closed-up grace, leaving
No trace, no answers. Just a huge deep music
In every corner of the street, the years.

FINISH LINE

Memories like heroes they never grow old
— Eric Bogle, 'Front Row Cowboy'

In the old black and white on my wall he's posing,
looking right at the lens, smiling, standing balanced
on the pedals, front wheel turned, facing down the concrete
banking of the track. That in itself is special.
Just the two of us that day, and he was good
to pose like that, world sprint champion, for a shy kid
in school uniform. 1950. He even said he liked
my bike, and let me lift his famous red Raleigh
with one young finger.

1993. Back there. The grandstand's gone where I used
to sit, near the finish line, and the track's crumbled
but is still there, the banking sheer and amazing.
Remnants even of painted advertisements for Reynolds Tubing.
I scramble down and walk around the ruined place
like some old actor in a condemned theatre listening
to the dead air. 5000 here for big meets. 2000 each
Tuesday. A trace of white paint at the finish line. Once
a friend and I sneaked onto the track and rode a lap,
but didn't dare attempt that fierce banking. Every week
I was there, met the touring pros, the world's best –
Van Vliet. Derksen. Paterson. Heid. The Frenchman.
Reg was the best by a tyre's width. Faster than a car
his last 200, legs pumping, bike whipping side to side.

1995. Back again, stupidly sentimental, deciding I'd get
a piece of that pink concrete for my desk. Gone. Gone.
The whole track gone. A university residence where it was.
So what do I do now? Reg would stall and fake, then
swoop off the banking and power past to the finish.
Stand still on the pedals until the other broke.
The muscles in his legs. A quiet smile. The fluent
power of what he was, of what I wanted to be like, what
all those thousands roared for. It was a place of wonder.
A place for the fastest in the world. Now it's dug under.
Now it's for students who've never heard of Reg Harris
(or the track, the crowds) who'll never know that a man
came here from Canada for a piece of concrete and went
home with nothing but heavy memory come alive.
What I was. What I am. The old dilemma. Trying to balance it.
In the photo he's wearing his World Champion jersey.
He and I, nothing can change us now.

I.

I thought I'd lost them. I was only twelve
After all, and much of consequence,
I like to think, has happened to me since those

Heady days. But here they are, rescued
From the depths of a storage box in our Calgary
Basement. Four of them. Musty. Slight foxing,

That old-book smell, but not bad for their age.
I dust them off, sit down and start to look,
Smiling. Good visitors, like surprise birds

Blown off course, not seen for years, but remembered.
Oliver Twist. Robinson Crusoe. Mr.
Midshipman Easy. Masterman Ready.

2.

Captain Marryat in my life again!
His name starts old currents flowing, breezy
Shivers of pleasure. I read. Born 1792,

Left school at fourteen – without too many prizes
I'd guess – joined the Navy as a midshipman,
Took part in 'more than fifty engagements',

Won honours and promotions, then suddenly
'Left the sea for literature'. Wrote 'many
Novels and other books'. No first name given.

Things float back – the tang of derring-do;
Reading late in bed. I start to remember
Plots, but it's more the feel of youthful weather.

3.

Nelson Classics. Blue covers with gold school crest.
Inside, a form signed by the High Master,
My name in black ink copperplate. Two were

For being top of the class, two for the 'Procter
Reading English Prize', this for reading
Out loud, with audience, some unseen passages

Of poetry to a teacher – Master, rather –
Which, I recall, I won because, with luck,
I didn't stumble over 'tintinnabulation

Of the bells'. (See me then – blue uniform. Shorts.
Room 22. Mr Lingard. Form 1C.
The High Master was made a Lord. Lingard died young.)

4.

It must have been easy in those days to choose
Prize books, give the same ones every year.
Old, no sex, a whiff of high adventure

To stir the blood (though not too much), a remedial
Dash of wholesome outdoor moral values,
A sweet long-standing deal with Nelson, I'm sure.

It would lead to fights today. I read Marryat
Before I hunkered into Dickens and Defoe,
And it all washes back as I scan the contents,

Each chapter summarized in short phrases.
(I hated that; it gave away the plot.)
And twelve seems real, my sailing off with Ready!

5.

And now I read, dip in, splash about in it.
Kind, God-fearing, strong and resourceful, Ready,
Above all a decent sort, saves the middle-

Class Seagrave family from shipwreck, helps
Them survive the desert island, lectures the kids
On God and Fate after each day's adventures.

Shrewd and practical, he's endearing, wise.
He foresees Africa superseding England
In power. Is kind to the black girl who calls him 'Massa',

Beats back aggressive 'savages' to save them all,
But dies, nobly of course, in the finest tradition.
'No surgeon can help, sir. I'll be in Eternity.'

6.

At twelve I didn't recognize clichés.
The Seagraves, shocked and stricken, gratefully
Wrap Ready in the ship's flag, are soon rescued,

And full of grief return to England, wise now,
Tempered. What should I do? Smile? Groan? Each
Day on the island ended with thanksgiving

But then the hero dies. It's a teasing lesson
For a callous lad, not harmful, I'm sure,
To swing around from joy to prayer to grief,

To celebrate braveness and kindnesses,
Certainties gone wrong, people learning.
Today it's condemned as 'colonial paradigm'.

7.

I'm grateful to the old sea dog. And not just
For a good read. His novels pushed me forward,
Led me to Hornblower, which led to Conrad,

To *Lord of the Flies*, to *Moby Dick*, to *Voss*,
And on it goes. I wouldn't want, myself,
To die for honour and country, fight spears

With calmness, wit, technology, have
To give thanks after every castaway day
For surviving, be called 'Massa', almost worshipped,

But, sentimental and wooden now, these books
Spoke from him to me, and helped me bring,
I think, some decencies to my calms and storms.

8.

Went back to the school to visit – a strange shore
Which welcomed me, though I felt small again.
Prizes are gone. A school bookstore sells new

Stuff. The daily singing of hymns has stopped,
And thanking our Founders. The place smells just the same.
Room 22. Lingard. The lost young faces.

A uniformed Prefect, I patrolled here once
To keep the place safe, the savage voices quiet.
Here we learned about Pacific islands.

There a boy fell down the stairwell. There
We changed for sports. Here saw plays. My island!
Blessed I grew until they called me ready.

9.

I look over my shoulder at that boy
Of twelve, steal his books, know it matters that he
Saved them, now that storms and distant islands

No longer give us pause, arrogant world tourists,
Though they should. We're dull-eyed, much too casual.
Can we be sure, Marryat keeps asking us,

That we know more now? That there's not some huge wave
Behind us, breaking, that will toss us, helpless,
Far up some lost beach with no blue uniform,

No kind hand to rescue us, give thanksgiving?
See Chapter 61: *Explanation* —
Ready dying — *Ready's Death* — *Arrangements.*

HEARING SIRENS
(for D. B. & the Café Hille, Andernach)

Driving by the river in the city,
A woman singing on the car stereo,
Dressed as usual in my Calgary skin,

Nothing special about any of it,
Then I'm back, without reason, suddenly
Back at a river-bend deep in Europe,

That famous rock on the Rhein, inside my early
Imperious self at one of the world's special
Places, however small I remember thinking

It looked at the time. The voice swims round the car.
What were those words about that place, the ones
We learned at school, and mocked, singing, 'Nothing

Could be finer than to study Heinrich Heine
In the mor–or–or–ning.' Stupid that I remember.
What were those words? *Ich weiß nicht was soll*

Es bedeuten Daß ich so traurig bin. [1]
That's *it*, I say aloud. The lines about
The Lorelei, her rock, that place of gawkers,

---

1. I don't know what it means that I am so sad.

Clicking shutters, and that young me with his life
Ahead, in his pack a brand new sixteen-hole
Hohner chromatic in its polished box.

Car engines, the Bow River, the stereo,
But I'm back there, stuck at that bend of the Rhein,
Though why there tonight and not New York, Paris,

Orkney, the London jazz club, Iowa City,
I can't understand. Or women, punts, and a soft
Grey, willow-rich river where once I played

That Hohner quietly, and talked and drank cold wine.
It's not my choice. That once-me, tanned and eager!
The voice in the car has become achingly soft.

Ein Märchen aus alten Zeiten – I recall it
Now, I think – *Das kommt mir nicht aus dem Sinn.* [2]
A voice over water, irresistible,

Pulling men out of their senses to that rock.
A siren sounds on 14th Street. And then
Another. And the voice is deep and clear

---

2. A legend/story from ancient times that does not come to me
   from the rational mind.

Filling the car, my eager puzzled head,
And the watery whisper and swish of tyres is nothing
But lovely, and I'm speeding up now, pushed

Or pulled by the years, or something, feeling good
And *traurig*, towards whatever's ahead, waiting,
And this present-me, wiser no doubt than that

Young one back across the years, is still
Not strong enough. More sirens. And I move forward
With all the others, one after another,

Tranced, hearing music, something strong and sweet
And strange I can't guess more about but don't
Avoid. Not sensible. But how passionate

The sweet voices in my mind, and I know,
Somehow, that all this will take some time
Before it stops, before it sorts itself out,

Before I can turn the wheel and steer for home.

DEPARTURE GATE
(For J.)

My son expects a sonnet in this book,
He tells me, grinning, as we shake hands. I
Say I don't have one planned, then catch a look
Of my father's face in his – the mouth, the eye –

And watch him stride away, through the big door
Where I can't follow. Oh son, at twenty-four
You don't know how important farewells are,
Or how they bring back things too hard to bear,

Grim things from which we know we can't recover.
Fly safely. I'll write, I promise. I turn away,
Remembering how it was when I was young

And things were always waiting, the journey over,
Not left behind, the way it feels today.
(Dad, since you died each day is tilted wrong.)

Depressing, the treeless village. Rows of grey
Houses pouring coal smoke, quiet dull-coated
Old women with string shopping bags at the shops,
A noisy, fuming 1950s bus,
A bent man walking, pulled by two slow dogs.
No grace or softness here. No laughter. Smoke.
Two small schools – Catholic and Protestant –
At morning break, pale children playing tag
In concrete playgrounds behind iron railings.
In one a teacher rings a handbell, shouts,
Bullies them into neat and equal lines.
Everything seems forty years adrift
And something's wrong. There's something out of balance.

I retreat into a graveyard, needing colour,
Drawn by the soft cut grass and bright flowers,
Stroll casually along a row of graves,
Start reading. Then I understand. Stone after
Stone explains it all – the grey village,
The smoke, the old quiet people. I walk and read,
One after another down each perfect row.
Buried in Whitehill Colliery. Killed in
An accident in Bilston Glen Colliery.
Trapped with his friends in Tunnel 30. Killed.
Buried. Accidentally killed. The smoke,
Thick incense, rises for them, down far down
Beneath their homes. So many. *Collapsed tunnel.*
Killed. Dead underground. Those houses were theirs,
Those were their relatives I saw – widows,
Children, grandchildren – for some died not long

Ago, though today the pits are closed and slag
Heaps and prettified ruins are all you see.
They've kept the village just the way it was,
As the dead would know it if they all came back,
Grimy, jostling, laughing, wanting a pint.
It wasn't meant, of course, but any change
Would seem a sacrilege to their descendants.

I walk further. A different line of stones.
Infant son. Infant daughter. Taken in childhood.
More of these than there should be, surely? I flinch
At one with fresh flowers on it. (Flowers grow
Better than children in this smoke-grey climate,
I think savagely, remembering my own
Children, near here, coughing their lungs to sleep.
That cold dampness. How far away we took them.)

Quickly turning from those two-foot graves,
I come to sons and husbands *Killed in the Great
War. Killed in World War Two.* Tough soldiers, I bet.
A lot from here, and this just one of the graveyards.
I walk on slowly, clenched hard. Bright birdsong
Wraps around me. Sweet mocking music.

More miners. More. More stones lovingly tended,
Half a mile or more above the bodies.
It frightens, the thought of so much depth in a tomb,
The way the earth closed up and left just names
Formed here in perfect lines, bells rung for them.
Those old women. The wrecked families. The lives

Inside those houses, offering up coal smoke.
And I come from miners – my father's family.
These deep dead ones would have heard about
Shotton in Durham. Somehow my line survived.
I cling to it, hoping the earth will hold me up.

Nearly at the gate, thinking I've made it,
When I'm done for by one last stone, unbearable
Only because of the others. I hear it spoken
In soft Scots. *Not goodbye, just goodnight dear.*
For miners, babies, soldiers, this last voice –
Simple, maudlin, terrible in its love.

                            Midlothian, 1993

The Bass Rock out to sea, sunlit white now,
And I think of how it was part of those holidays
After the war, staying in North Berwick,

In exotic Scotland. That shining reminds me how
We took sightseeing boats, on the calmer days,
Around the Rock, two hours, seeing North Berwick

From the sea, watching the feeding gannets, how
They'd plunge a hundred feet just to amaze
Us as we rocked on the Forth, out from North Berwick.

And then the Bass Rock jetty, and then how
We climbed, avoiding nests, all in a daze
Of shriek, stink, and magic. Back to North Berwick

Triumphant, films used up, and it was how
My father managed it, far beyond my praise,
That I think of now, revisiting North Berwick,

Back here, without a father, in North Berwick,
No pleasure boats in the harbour these run-down days,
And the pool's abandoned. Only the birds dive now.

In the churchyard, at the grave,
I bend to see if east winds have left
it readable. He in the 1930s, his wife,
my grandmother, when I was eight.
I just remember her face, have a few
photographs. She knew this place so well.
And here I am.

I go inside. It's empty. Air stale.
Up in the pulpit I look around,
pretend to be my grandfather, the vicar,
sixty-five years ago. His wife, I think,
and children (my mother and aunt)
would listen from the front pew.
Silent, I talk to them there.

Up at the altar rail, turning,
I pretend to be my father
and I walk down the short aisle
my dark-haired bride on my arm.
Or I could be my uncle making
the same smiling walk, my mother's
fair-haired sister beside me,
holding her bright bridal flowers.
Two walks into all our futures!
More to it all than they knew then,
though they'd have been full of hope.
My mother and aunt. Widows now, old,
in a warmer town, remembering.

At the old stone font
I lift the heavy lid and think
of being myself, screaming right here,
so I've been told, as the water
shocked my fuzzy skull.

Back at the lectern, and why am I
so restless, I pretend to be my uncle,
vicar, strangely, after my grandfather died,
as well as his daughter's husband,
and I hear him saying gentle words here.
I smile softly for him,
so recently dead.

What would they think, my haunting
their place like this?

Suddenly two oldish women come in,
weighted down with flowers and fruit,
to decorate for the Harvest Festival.
Lifelong attenders, most amazingly
they know about my family and this place,
make me tell them what happened
to everyone, where the years took us.
You must bring your boys here,
the quiet one said.
This is your family's special place.

Because I'm tall they ask me
to put some bread above the altar.
I stand on a chair, stretch up
to the ledge below the coloured glass,
prop two decorated loaves high there,
one on each side.

Reaching, I do it for remembrance.
This one for you, grandfather.
This for you, uncle.
Bright flowers for all the others.

And before I leave, the colours have been
arranged and strewn all round the place
until the stone itself turned sweet.

My grandmother, the family elder, stood
Here that day, her husband, recently buried
In the grass outside, not twenty yards from her.

Strange emotions, I'd guess, it must have stirred
In them, the body and the baby so close,
But they crowded round this font, watching the show,

As Christopher Stephen Wiseman was named and blessed,
Validated, readied to go forth.
I'm sure she prayed for me, that vicar's widow.

I'm sure they all did in their different ways.
I'm sure they smiled as I screeched at the cold water,
Was hurriedly passed back to my mother's arms.

Today I'm alone. Same church. Same font. And I think
All that crowded family's dead. All gone
But two, my grandmother's children in their nineties,

And they will never come to this place again.
All gone, and my life well along, my children
Married, thinking of children of their own.

I look at it, the dark oak lid with its black
Iron ring, the stone carved all around –
Suffer the Little Children to Come unto Me

For of Such Is the Kingdom of Heaven – and I feel
A weight, as if I've been transformed to some
Sort of reluctant representative,

Helpless, filled with demanding generations.
The oldest man. The family patriarch now.
But how much wiser than when I was that baby?

I lift the heavy lid. Two inches of old
Stale water lying at the bottom – hardly
The stuff of legend. I smile, though why in God's

Name I should, I don't know. Between me and my car
Lies my grandmother, next to her husband,
And how have her prayers for me turned out, and why,

I wonder, do I walk past her so quickly?

Sewerby, Yorkshire

The two of us
Are at your stone,
Your wife and I.
She can't come alone

Now but she's brought
A flower to leave,
Long-stemmed, rich red,
A memento of love.

Wind takes the leaves
In this grey place.
Stooped, frail, she tries
To reach you, face

Intent, but she
Can't reach to give
You her flower,
Can't reach you to give

Even this small thing.
I stretch and place
It for her, see
Her crumbling face

Pitifully
Frustrated. We stand
Together near you,
My arm around

Her, understanding
Something of this
But not enough.
It never is.

We'll both go on
As best we can,
Father, husband,
O much missed man,

Leaving with you
The bright bright red
On your stone, and much
That can't be said.

I sit with her and they fill
My head. All the time they seem to get louder
As they chatter, so I shout above them.
A quiet room, but never still,

Not with the clocks. We talk, her kind
Eyes carefully watching my lips to help
The hearing-aid as the enormous rattling
Insistence grows. They're very kind

To me here, she says, trying
To reassure, to ease my worries, but how,
My jet-lagged head wonders, with four of the eight
In their nineties, are the bad thoughts, when lying

Here at night, even though she's what
Is called hale and hearty, the healthiest
In the place, coped with? How, with this
Demented angry commotion in her room, not

At all synchronized, as the two clocks
And her loud old watch race each other
So fast I think they're going to deafen me?
The room is square, a concrete annexe,

And the din has nowhere to escape to. I
Can't even see the clock by her bed, but three
Sets of time's crazy teeth – my watch is silent
And I'm glad – living here in possession and in my

Ears begins to turn me silly. Scared. Then
I realize that of course she can't hear
Them in her gentle silent world, doesn't have
To fear them, come to terms. Reassuring, that. Again

We talk. Once a year across the ocean,
So a lot between us, a lot to say, and she
With more than ninety years now to recall for me.
Anecdotes. Feelings. She seems contented. Alone

In here, she reads and watches TV,
Plays music, writes letters. Joins the others
For meals and in the lounge. Reads to the blind one.
This time matters to me – I hold it closely –

And to her, as the old years slip softly by.
We talk of how it used to be
With us, as the clocks scurry all round, and once,
Strangely, she mentions my

Big clock (the one I'll inherit),
The loud chimer, presented to her father
Long before my time, which sounded off
Every quarter hour – I still have it

In my heartbeat – of my growing up, and
How it needed so much sheer strength to turn
The big brass key each week as it slowed.
Too big for in here, she says, and her hand

Arthritic now, though its great slow
Deep tick, I think, might calm and balance
the frenzy of these others, stop making me
Think of just a few yards to go

In some desperate sprint, as they seem
To fight and jostle and try to run each other down.
Three clocks. Two people. Outnumbered. And although
There's so much love here, and we dream

Aloud, chat, wonder at how we've all turned out,
About myself as child, my children, all time's changes,
And how I'll come again next year, retired
(Early) by then and puzzled, I expect, about

How best to pass my time, this is more
Sound than I can stand, more threat, and getting
Worse by the minute, by the second.
I make to leave. Hug her. Open the door.

I'll be back tomorrow, everything willing.
The clocks tick on. I know the clocks won't stop.
Alone, she sits with time, his furious chatter
Loose, her quiet room filling.

1.

Machine guns were the worst,
sweeping the bare mud in arcs,
though marching forward from the trenches,
bayonets fixed, attracted everything
else they had too. One massacre. Another
massacre. Noise enough to kill.
And you there. But before the subaltern's
whistle sent everyone over the top again,
a shell exploded in the trench, blowing
you like paper against the boards,
ending the war for you.
And other things.

2.

I hold an invoice sent to you
ten years after that, the date, everything,
handwritten, copperplate, in pen.
I only found it recently in a book
your daughter gave me.
An impressive heading:
29/9/26. W. & G. Foyle, Limited.
Booksellers, second-hand and new.
121–5 Charing Cross Road.
Over a million volumes always in stock.
Telephone Gerrard 3251 (2 lines).
It looks good. Has kept its life well.
Survived.

3.

I try to understand this.
In five months, starting July 1, 1916,
415,000 'British and Empire' soldiers were killed
at the Somme. More than 20,000 the first day alone.
Around 600,000 Germans. More
than half a million others wounded. Wave after wave
they marched towards the wire and died.
Trenches often knee-deep in mud and water.
A few tree stumps, leafless.
Bodies floating in pools of old craters.
The dead laid in rows or buried where they were.
(Only later the precise enormous cemeteries.)
Five months, the Somme. A million dead.

4.

Men in their nineties on TV, remembering.
The screams, one said. Men screaming
and nobody could get to them.
Collecting the discs and pay books from the dead,
said another, carrying them in emptied sandbags.
Men crying like children, said the oldest.
Terrified. Clawing at their faces. Gone mad.
And they remembered writing home
on wet and muddy scraps of paper,
and singing 'Wait Till the Sun Shines Nellie'
before they went over the top again.
His friend's head blown off next to him
in the trench, said one, still grieving,
seventy-five-year-old tears in his eyes.

5.

You comforted the dying, prayed
over the dead and closed their eyes
before that shell got you.
Your hands on all those faces. Blood. Dirt.
You held services before the attacks
from your Communion set, silver vessels
in a battered carrying box. Wine. Wafers.
An old wooden folding table for an altar.
Rough bass voices roaring hymns
in the desolation of the mud fields,
trying to drown the guns.
The last time
many of them would ever sing.
'O God of Battles' was one prayer.
The broken landscape. Open mouths.
Screaming shells. Screaming men. Screams.
Wide desperate eyes. These never left you,
gentle man.

6.

After all that, you hid deep
in the Yorkshire countryside, lost
yourself in the small peace of villages.
The country vicar. Safe now.
The Rev. E. Rigby, Ganton vicarage,
Ganton, nr. Scarborough, it says.

Tells us the book you sent for –
Hearnshaw, Social and Political Ideas.
Six and Threepence, postage Sixpence.
Total Six and Ninepence.
Not cheap then, and I wonder
what ideas you were hoping to find
to quiet your mind in that dark house
in the trees – oh yes, I've been to see it –
in the burble of pigeons, the song of thrushes.
Did living with that wound make you
want to think about why people fight?
Did reading drown out the screaming?
Tell you what is just and politic?

7.
And one remembered a seventeen-year-old
wandering, sobbing, away from his trench.
They led him gently back, then shot him.
(Three-hundred shot for desertion at the Somme.)
Did you have to be there at executions
to pray and comfort? Please not.
Most cracked up in the bombardments,
day and night shelling up to a week.
Screamed. Went quiet. Wandered off like toddlers.
'Lack of Moral Fibre', the army called it.
Abnormal behaviour for a soldier.

8.

Telegraphic address Foylibra,
Westcent, London. Technology
Humanized by the Latin, not like those
telegraphs in the killing fields.
And that huge shop a family concern –
Directors W. A. Foyle, G. S. Foyle –
offering personal attention to customers,
as to a dying man in mud, reaching
for help, for anyone, for you.
Books purchased – a single volume
to a library. One man in a shell-hole
Or scores of bodies laid in rows together.
Sorting bags full of paybooks.
Over a million volumes always in stock.
No invoice from the Somme, but you paid
with interest, on the instalment plan.
It took years.

9.

I imagine you in Ganton vicarage,
All the bright birds whistling like bullets,
and you with this book, looking past the pages.
I imagine a shotgun blast by some local,
Blazing away at pigeons, and you shaking.
I doubt if you spoke about the things you'd seen.
You lived so quietly, your daughters say.

10.

Blood. Water. Screaming. Shell-holes. Gas. Death sounds.
Five months of 'the great offensive' underground
Or seeking cover. Five months. A million dead.
And at the end they'd won five miles of mud.

11.

Birds and bullets singing in your head,
shells in trenches, by old village trees,
bodies lying, uniformed or feathered,
twitching in mud or soft grass.
And you trying to clear your dreams
with Hearnshaw's *Social and Political Ideas*,
your dreams where living things kept falling
down and calling for you. All the time,
in Ganton village or the Somme, calling for you.
Back home, for months you wouldn't close
the bedroom windows. Wouldn't be shut in.
Sometimes your wife slept in her winter coat.

12.

My Foyle's invoice from this year is small,
two colours, fashionably unpunctuated.
Headline – *The World's Greatest Bookshop* –
less stylish than yours. A different world.
This bill must be produced in the event
of any query regarding purchase.
And the address not quite the same –
113–119 Charing Cross Road.

But they've grown, brought in reinforcements.
Now it's *Stock of over five million volumes.*
I paid seven pounds for a paperback.
I was there, by chance, on the 75th anniversary
of the second day they realized the horror of it.
Fewer than half the 120,000 returned unharmed.
The day they picked up 20,000 books.

13.
I hope the dying learned something from you,
if that is ever possible. I hope
you learned something from this dull red book,
because each year, at your quiet gravestone,
swept by a vicious wind straight from Europe,
I learn nothing. I reach out. Nothing.
Just the loss. Just the silent scream of loss.
A shell, a book, a long-dead wounded grandfather
who never knew me.
Invoice number R2847.

AT THE BOMBER COMMAND MEMORIAL
(Lincoln Cathedral)

Enormous, high above the city,
this place was their signpost home.

Not much chance, and they knew it.
Fifty-seven thousand RAF bomber crew dead.
Ten thousand planes destroyed. One in three.
I must write something. But who for?
Their wives, girl-friends, parents, children, I think.
Today it's just history to so many, distant
as the Civil War, the Conquest, the Fire of London.

Words. I need to speak. But what can I say
about Dresden, Hamburg, Lübeck, Köln,
that I can or can't say about London,
Hull, Exeter, Coventry? All the shattered places?
They say in Hamburg people just caught fire
in the streets, and I can't say anything.
I think I write for all the bodies everywhere.
The dead, rather. Many were never bodies.

The sun through stained-glass windows blinds me.
Says yes or no. Says fire and death. Says peace
and safe return. Says sorry and thanks.
The colours blind me. Blind me
like searchlights.

The choir begins to practise. Young voices
soaring and darting in this enormous tomb,
climbing higher and higher, clear and sweet.

Outside, I hurl words up as high as I can,
hard and urgent at the blankness of the same sky
where men threw up, pissed themselves,
created firestorms beyond belief. Died. Died.
One in three.

I look at the sun on the stunning white towers.
The old builders believed in a fiery devil,
created magnificence to spite him,
never thinking they built a pointer
for men's red-rimmed arrival from hell,
their landing heavily on the earth.

LONESOME PINE BREAKDOWN
(For J. Z.)

This pinewood is dying. Age. Disease.
Trees are death-grey, some fallen,
some leaning as they try to stand,
some propped up in another's arms, waiting
for the wind to pull them away and down.

No surge. No juice. Dead twigs clutch
and stab you as you walk. Brittle. Sharp.
They don't smell of trees. There are no birds
feeding, nesting, finding shelter.
Each year I find more of them down,

favourites I've watched, not thought about.
I come here for health and quiet, to tap
what juices I have left, to pull
around myself what it is I lack,
grasp and keep some shining that I need.

Now, instead, I see the reluctant fallings,
hear restless creaking death rattles,
marvel at how the weakest still hang on.
What is there here for me? I know.
The trees are saying hurry, hurry,

we've been telling you every year,
showing you with our lives. We can't
help this, they're saying, it's over sooner
than even we thought it would be.
And we were old before you were young.

LAMENT IN LATE WINTER
(J.M., d. 1997)

The clouds have filled and hang above us here.
Snow falls on ice. The winter will not end.
And now this, too. The pity and the fear.
The clouds have filled and hang above us here.
We slide around, trying to hold on. Here
We stop, but we'll find spring, or at least pretend,
Though the clouds have filled and hang above us here.
Snow falls on ice. This winter will not end.

Last drive in Britain, five hours to the airport
On a road much taken, its signs always bringing
My smiles, suggesting richness that I miss,
Things to look for, deep, important to me.
And I've been celebrating my mother's ninetieth.
Fowles' Lyme Regis, the Hardy graves, Golding's
Spire, Austen's tomb, this road has given joy,
Cheered me, seductive as any snow-filled woods.
But today it's not to be borne. I see the signs,
Note some new ones, but feel reduced. Gaunt
Inside, yet full, I'm heavy on the throttle.

baby rabbits for sale – old people crossing – sheep hurdles –
flower festival – public bridleway – pick your own fruit – loose
chips – duck race on sunday – family beer garden – polo next left –
free range eggs – whole scottish kippers – heavy horses – 16th
century farm – lurgishall winery – salty monk hotel – fruit – come in –

Just a few days ago that other drive,
Starting near the distant gloom of Culloden,
The battlefield ragged grass, boulders, low sky,
A small cairn. Dark frightening desolation,
Not like the tourist glitz of the Custer memorial,
The planted order of those miles of crosses,
Tended and gentle, in France. My happy mother
ninety years old on April the 16th.
Culloden 250 on April the 16th.
Well over a thousand killed in the massacre,
The day after Cumberland's birthday party.
(Artillery. Muskets. Swords. Terrible woundings.)

Then driving past Perth I see the *Dunblane* sign.
March, that was, before my mother's birthday.
Dismayed, belly acid, I slow, confused,
Then drive on southward. Suddenly *Lockerbie
1 mile.* In one day. Too much. Signs everywhere,
Pointing. I cross into England. Stop. Worn out.
I have to read to children the next day.

*three cups hotel – eggs self service – roman villa – open – pedigree
nubian goats – puddletown – tolpuddle – affpuddle – strawberries –
come in – fancy bantams for sale – parking – animal hotel – open –
great working of steam engines – test river – fruit – pick your own –*

Should I have stopped at Dunblane, gone to graves,
Somehow paid tribute? The whole world sent flowers
Which lined the streets and overflowed the town.
Schoolkids in Calgary sent cards and letters there.
The five-year-old faces. One of them – Charlotte Dunn –
Sticks, but I don't know why. I had no daughter.
My sons, five, coming from school, unbuttoned
Shirts, untied shoes, happy, kicking stones.
The teacher, too, unable to protect.
The gods defend her, says Albany, and then
Lear enters with Cordelia dead in his arms.
And PanAm 103, its painted cockpit
On the grass at Lockerbie. Eight years already.
Broken metal raining on the town
Like something from deep in the Old Testament.
Two hundred and seven dead. The sky torn open.
Something has me by the throat, but miles,
Still long miles to go along this road.

delicious home cooked meals – bedding plants – stables – donkey
sanctuary – point to point – baby swans hatching – the sussex stud –
friary press – army firing range – pick all you want – watch for red flag –

I can't drive fast enough. Do I want the airport
And the flight back to Canada over Scotland,
Or just to get off roads, stop driving this car,
Seeing signs? How did I pass so much
Death in one day and keep going and keep going?
The sun is full. Birthdays and the dead
Are tense in my mind. Birds sing. Hedgerow scent
Sweetens the car. Flowers. Charlotte Dunn.
Children placing wildflowers on the coffins.

allhallows girls school – school fête – children play free – children
on road – beware children – schoolchildren crossing – children –

Crossing what once was their great sustaining kingdom,
Their children lost to them, unnatural death
All round, Gloucester happens to meet old Lear,
Mind overturned, dressed in coloured flowers.
He wants to kiss his hand. Let me wipe it first,
Lear says. It smells of mortality. Foolish
Fond old men, blind and crazed. The land is deep
With the calling dead. I know. I've passed among them.

1996

APRIL ELEGY
(Sam Selvon, d. 1994)

I call my mother on her birthday, the way
I always do. Eighty-eight this time and so

Alive, thank God. I can hear her smile. She may,
She says, for this is morning there, go

To the shops later. We talk about the way
She feels, the way England is, a chance to go

And visit her sister. Family talk. The way
We do. I miss her. I miss others. Go

Back when I can. You went a different way,
Sam, old smiler – this time you were asked to go

Back to Trinidad, famous there now, way
Past time. And you were pleased, you said, to go.

I sometimes met you in the shops here, the way
People meet, and we talked of how it was to go,

After the war, to London, alone, and the way
You survived, the jobs, how you made money go

Further in your long exile. The way
You told it, you'd enjoy yourself and go

Collect people and places there, learn the way
You had to write them, make them speak, go

On giving time to lives, pointing a way.
Why were we both in exile? Why did we go

Walkabout from our roots? We discussed the way
Of the world, journeying, the push to go.

You stop on my mother's birthday – nice the way
You did that, like a writer – more shops to go

To, more good talk untalked, and see, way
Across the ocean, this spring day, she will go,

My mother, healthy, eighty-eight, the way
She does, to her shops. You never said you'd go.

Never told me that, like this, you'd go.

Black cars on the white street ready to leave.
Slowly he starts to go out of our life.
Passive Chinese faces. No tears. Going
To bury the old man in the frozen ground.
Freeze him in. Go deep for those old bones.

I think of the life, the cruel tearing apart.
Came here in the 1920s. Worked. Worked.
Bought the store. Nineteen sixty-three
He went back home to bring his wife and daughter.
Two short visits back in forty years.

Here, his wife never stepped outside the house.
Never once. Died in 1970, old.
His daughter never learned English. Never
Tried. Just 'Hi' as she smiled and bobbed to us
Over the fence for sixteen years. Cooked. Washed.

Walked one step behind him on the street.
Her husband in Vancouver, but she stayed here
For the old man. Had a daughter. Grandchildren.
And always King Loo working in his store,
Eyes failing. Each Christmas he brought chocolates

Sitting in our house for fifteen minutes,
Cigarette dangling from his lips, smiling.
Jagged English. The neighbourhood – 'New China
Boys. Hong Kong boys. Not real China boys.'
Contempt there for some lack of pride, of class.

Behind him. Always one step. Everyone.
The old man, his torn life strong in the whiteness.
How he made Christmas rich for our children.
The cars glide away, one just behind the next.
Even on that day King's store stays open.

Work. Work. How could a man rip apart his life
That way? His great-grandchildren flourish here,
Albertans now. The black cars take away
Our neighbour. I grieve him as he disappears.
Winter. The heart's weather. The tearing over.

KIND WORDS (A LAMENT)

That July of 1991
I was in a hotel room in London
when the radio turned me cold.
The actress Lee Remick has died
in California. Among her many films ...
I had a theatre ticket for that night,
and went, guilty and heavy.

We were exactly the same age
I learned from the obituaries.

Damn damn you were gorgeous – pouty
and flaunting it in *Anatomy of a Murder*,
later just sexy, at home in your body.
You lived for years in England,
could play English or American,
Joe Orton or made-for-TV cosy.
Strong, full-bodied woman, you
were different from the others.
(Brightness, dignity, something like that.)
Your voice was molasses hardening.

The same age. I avoid the mirror.
I won't think about your last year,
your belated star on the sidewalk
when you could hardly stand.
No. Not that scene. Never.

Home, I look hard into the black
and white glossy you sent me –
young, hair-shining, half a smile.
A clear bold hand, as it would be with you.
For Chris, with love, and thanks
for the kind words!

From my wall your eyes follow me,
brighten my room, blaze inside me.
I write these words with love
(oh yes, yes, yes) and thanks
for the kind hours, the years we had.

MAYDAY

Old rituals cluster round the first of May –
Bathing in the morning dew, gathering
Flowers, declaring love. The famous day
For lovers, for touching hands, for dallying.

Officially you were Alberta's worst ever
Mass murderer. And only thirty-two
When you did it. Killed four girls on Prince's
Island bridge that day. All young. You
Just stopped and threw your baby in the river –
The Bow raging with run-off – and the two
Young ones after her. Then you. Then you
Holding the oldest, six, as close to you
As any mother could. Nobody could reach you.

The first of May for love, for the heart's new season.
For hands. For holding. For what love feels like.

Everybody tried to find a reason.
They settled on depression, finally,
For what else could it be with your plans
To travel, your big house? And certainly
It was not that you didn't love your daughters,
Or that you grieved because you'd borne no son.

Mayday is for bathing in the dew,
The day for holding one another close.
The day for love.
                    And what, that day, for you?

Calgary was shocked. But see what you'd done –
You'd carefully wrapped one daughter's fingernails
So she couldn't scratch her chicken pox.

O Mayday for loving, where the river bends.

H. B., May 1, 1979

What can be done here in this grass
Enclosure, watching them get
Their food and eat? What are we
To do but keep our eyes from gaping
At their bodies, broken, boneless,
Hooped, tottering almost over?
One takes six-inch steps at amazing
Speed. One lopes with giant strides,
Uncontrolled, flopping. One eats
Ice cream from a hot-dog bun,
Then goes for more, sticky and dripping
In the heat. Some stare at us.

Many are not long for the world,
And I've sometimes seen the older ones
In the cemetery, shakily looking
At the exact place they know they'll lie,
The sad carcasses of them at least,
While the strong person inside they've
Always known is really them
Will at last go free and fly.

What can be done? It's frightening
To see this much pain, deformity,
In one place, and some of us
Giggle nervously, and some
Won't ever come to the barbecues.
We try very hard, walk around
And talk and laugh about the cooking
As if we were ward visitors.
They should be in an institution,
Someone whispers, then we realize
They are, and a better one than those
We know about. And if they have
Come to terms with their cartoon bodies,
Could they have things to tell us about
Our pains, our hurting heads and hearts,
Those things gone wrong despite our upright
Bones? We finish our food and leave,
The cool and dark of evening coming,
We without an abbey or a god,
Not even knowing where we'll lie.

St. Peter's Abbey, Saskatchewan

I. (1903)

I'm here. What shall I do? I need help.
There are so few of us and the land is waiting.
What can I do? I must lead now, must hope
To see further, deeper, behind this weather,
Just as I saw that here we had to stop.
I see a great wheel lying on this land
And inside it all the faithful. They build farms
And churches all across this plain. Yes,
And in the centre of the great land-wheel
Will be a new abbey, a new landmark,
Bigger, I think, than I have even thought
Of yet, God willing. (Let me not be proud.)
An abbey. *Ja!* An abbey like in Europe,
With corn and potatoes, fishponds, loving Sisters
To cook, a bell for prayers, and a school, oh yes,
A school to teach good English to us all.
And I see avenues of trees. Paths. Flowers.
I see much, but do I know enough to start?
If this is vanity may the Lord forgive.
O lieber Gott! I see a whole colony
Lying across this land worshipping. But
I have time to start only. The journey
Has been long. I'm far from help. But I hope.
From Italy, Blessed Saint, and Germany,
The work continues and is always passed on.
These words I write on my mind in the year of Our Lord
1903. I need help. He will give it.
A book is in my head, with big pictures!

II. (1993)

You were close, Bruno Doerfler, though even you
Would be amazed if you walked here today –
New computers running huge presses,
Tens of thousands of newspapers each week,
A gym, arena, running track, weight room,
College labs, the latest farm machinery
Efficient and humming. The mission in Brazil
Would have pleased you, old traveller, and the peace
Here still, in spite of the new things. You'd grieve
For this world, I know, but see a challenge here,
Another page to turn, though the final drifting
Away of the Sisters, the old age of the monks,
Would disturb you. And the loss of the Latin words.
And what would you think of the casual work clothes,
The constant money-raising, visitors at Mass,
Marriage therapy, evening ball games?
But even you, turn-of-century austere,
Would be well pleased by the fine special place
Where you lie, some fifty white stones now
Gathered round you there in neat rows.
Here, I think, is the centre of the wheel.
You at the front, flowers growing in soft
Grass over you, tended each evening,

And birdsong everywhere in the warm breeze
Loud enough to dance your bones, old man,
Underneath your dark grey marble stone.
R'mus BRUNO DOERFLER O.S.B.
Monasterii St. Petri Abbas 1 et inter
Fundatores Coloniae Sti Petri princeps.
You stepped out of those myths of quest and journeys
When you came here and knew enough to stop.
You left the future and wrote yourself inside it.

St. Peter's Abbey, Saskatchewan

Late breakfast in the gas-station restaurant
And already I'm blessing the air conditioner.
The regulars are sitting at two tables,
The young ones and old ones, all in jeans, check shirts,
Baseball caps. They dismiss me with a glance.
The old ones flirt mildly with the waitress,
Who's more their age, drink coffee, smoke. This each
Morning, I guess – jokes, easiness together –
The generations different only in lines
On the skin, the leg-jiggling tautness of the young.

Six nights now. Six nights of my life I've spent
In Rosetown, driven through the heated bowl
Of prairie, stopped where this place is, and slept.
You are foreign here it says to me each time.
Leaves an impression other places don't.

A few stores, churches, a rink, the John Deere dealer's
Compound, gas stations, three motels. I saw
No movie house. Walking, you cross scrubby
Dirt lots between buildings. It's small. Travellers
Pull in for a washroom, drink and gas, then leave.
Only a few stop, as I do, but two
Years ago there was a wedding party
In the biggest motel – twenty or so men
In powder-blue tuxes, cream frilly shirts,
The women in pink, white high heels, heavy
Lacquered hair. They milled around the lobby,
Some drinking beer from the bottle. A little girl
In pink wet the carpet. Her mother slapped her.

The waitress wears pink panties under her white.
The men laugh in the smoke. I look outside.
Huge grain elevators. The fields, due south,
Over the tracks, already shuddering.
I'm not real. I'm out of my element.

I look at the young ones and wonder what it's like
To grow up in Rosetown, here, bare to the weather,
At a random crossroads. Is there a library?
A pool? Those soft things that shape you, where are they
At this map-point, this dusty coincidence
Where two straight highways meet, stop a moment,
Then disappear into four blank horizons?
I need to know where epiphanies come from here.
Fucking snob, I tell myself. Best go.
I don't like my thoughts. I'm not me. Never am,
Here in Rosetown where I'm drawn to stop.

What do I want? I guess I want to know
About dancing, music lessons, poetry,
First ideas about God, the young heart
Opening to paintings, concerts, theatre,
All the things I knew, and my friends too.
Were we just lucky seeing plays and operas?
Is Rosetown all the world except where we were?
Here, of course, first kisses, the secret throb
Of early sex, alcohol, winning a fight,
Dating, the first car. But is that enough?
Growing up in Rosetown haunts me. Births,
Weddings, deaths, but tenderness? And grace?
Is elegance something human beings need?

Again I say no to more coffee. She shrugs.
The young crowd leaves. I watch the old ones now.
Where does their laughter come from? I'll recall
Their faces, though I don't exist for them.
Why? The waitress sits down at their table.
One of them puts his hand on her thigh and strokes it.
She removes it only after she's finished lighting
A cigarette and putting the pack away.
Her face shows nothing. This is what they do.
It scares me. It's not what I do. What do I do?

I pay, meet the wall of heat, start the car.
Six nights in eight years. Rosetown's a pretty name.

A few miles down the Saskatoon highway,
Near Zealandia, a jacked-up Chevy
With fat tyres and crackling chrome mufflers
Passes me with a roar, and rocks my car,
Huge speakers thumping bass like artillery.
I recognize them. It's the young crowd,
The restless ones from the cafe, now drinking cans
Of beer as they race towards the morning sun.
Poor bastards, I think. What's life here got for them?

Then one leans out, looks back at me. Slowly,
Obscenely, happily, he gives me the finger.

THE DUCHESS TAKES THE WATERS, 1732

As coquette as if she were 18, and as rampant as if she were drunk
Lord Hervey on the Duchess of Marlborough, 1731

Dear Journal, 'tis the Hour to write, I see,
But O, Duke, would that I could talk with Thee!
My dear departed John, I am now old,
No longer comely, flush'd, handsome and bold.
If you're up There, look down and pity Me
In this rough Place beside a rougher Sea.
This private Book is such a Comfort here
(Though when I die I'll burn it, never fear.)
I stay in Scarb'ro, taking healing Waters
Among the *Nouveau-riche*, and common Daughters
Of blunt Tradesmen, who speak outlandishly
And giggle undemurely by the Sea.
(There *are* Ladies of low Nobilitie
But most have brought with them their Familie.)

NOTE: Sarah, Duchess of Marlborough, one of England's most influential women, visited Scarborough Spa in 1732. The details in the poem are taken from a letter she wrote to her granddaughter detailing her miserable lodgings, the lack of good company, the Ochre-playing young men and their dogs. 'The Spaw', she wrote, 'is Horrid'. The only invented part is that of Dick Dickinson's 'Peeping Tom' proclivities, for which I have no evidence, though we know that his curiously shaped body, his pet monkey and his dog induced more than a passing interest in some female Spa patrons.

From this I would be gone, except I'm sure
That being here will help effect some Cure.
The Waters, mull'd and Quaff'd with Wine, drunk slow
At Table, or elsewhere, impart a Glow.
I like to think that's Proof of certain Pow'rs
Which make it worth the Waste of precious Hours.
But still I must endure this Lodging House;
My Bed, I vow, is home to Flea and Louse.
Each Night, my Duke, I wake to Bark and Bray
Of Dogs penn'd up by Bucks who sleep all Day.
They spend the Nights at Cards and swilling Port.
Outside my Window these Hounds have their Sport.
They mount each other as I toss and turn,
And Sleeping Draughts are useless as I burn.
At his Spaw, Dick Dickinson, a Cripple,
Lusts for money, tries to glimpse a Nipple.
My Duke – I'm not mistook – his hot damp eyes
Linger on our Bodies, judging Size.
Into the dreadful Room we Ladies use
I've seen him peer, while we change Dress or Shoes,
Remove our Petticoats, apply Lotion
To dry out Skin from this accursed Ocean.
(The Lack of curtains is, I'm sure, his Notion.)
Young Wives and Fisher-girls – it's an Affront –
All gaze upon my bodie, Back and Front,
And giggle at my A_e, and T_ts, and C_t.
(Oh Duke, You us'd to breathe those Words to Me!
When You were full of Ardour it inflam'd Thee!)

The peasant Girls upset me much, my Dear;
I'm wrinkl'd when I'm stripp'd of costlie Gear.
Their skin is young and soft, their hair is black.
(I'll bet the Gov'nor meets them in the Back.)
I hate being display'd for common Girls
With horrid Accents as they pin salt Curls.
A Glass of Water more and then Adieu
To this grey Spaw, the Sea, the Fishwives too.
My Carriage waits, tomorrow I'll fare forth,
I never wish again to see the North.
I stretch my tir'd old Body in my Bed
And, Duke, I think of certain Things we did!
If only this were thirty Years ago,
Tomorrow Night would be both hot and slow!
Oh Sir, you'd flush and pant to hear me tell
Of bodies, white and firm, at Scarb'ro's Well.
I'd give you Pleasure, ere I pinch'd the Wick,
With hot Hounds, hairy Tradesgirls, crippl'd Dick!

SOCCER COACH

You've taught them all you can,
practised and practised with them.

Now, at the game, you watch, helpless,
head full of silent curses –

Shoot the fucking thing!
Pass it, you half-witted wanker!

For God's sake tackle him
you ugly misbegotten little turd! –

as their sun-tanning parents smile at you,
proud of their twelve-year-olds,

applauding every ridiculous mistake.
And you smile back, smile back, smile back.

Through the shattered gates they pour,
Theorists, post-feminists and more.
Revised history is on their side
And so they spread their banners wide –
Radicalize and feminize now!
Subvert the canon, that sacred cow
Of Dante, Chaucer, Shakespeare, Donne,
Which of course is male oppression,
And, worse, realistic, not avant-garde.
(And sometimes, perhaps, a bit too hard?)
Self-satisfied they bond and claim
That all is text, a language-game.
Reality and goodness? All
That meaning-stuff is past recall.
Now books are just to back up theory,
Or promote the cause of certain dreary
Groups of marginals – a solid bet
If little's published on them yet,
And not much on the Internet.
They triumph, for the frightened men
Dare not oppose with voice or pen.
Othered, or worse, the one who tries,
For to argue is to colonize.
People of colour, Derrida, late Plath,
Cixous, Foucault, the garden path.
All else is wrong politically,
And that is what they dare not be.
They take six months to learn the jargon
Of obscurity, then they're far gone
In a neo-speak that's all their own

And the inmates get to run the home.
Sad humanists slink home to write
Their realistic books at night,
Or, if they're male and white, not gay,
To calculate retirement pay.
How do new theories of narrative
Reveal to us how people live?
Or queer theory tell us why
Some lines of poetry make us cry?
To them such questions are passé –
Discredited universality –
And deconstructing works of art
Instead of feeling them is smart.
Such solidarity in rabble,
Sustained by complacent psychobabble.
(Thank God for Updike, Munro, Drabble!)
One thing is sure – if there's a heaven,
These zealots will never be forgiven
For reducing people more and more
And using poetry as a whore.
Prostituting works of art
Does damage to the human heart.
They haven't quite killed that off yet,
But look out, the agenda's set.

ive never kept kleenex in my office before but now there are tears
students dropping english hurt confused frustrated not getting
what they hoped they like novels and poems do i understand yes i
say but i dont try to change their minds theyre ten yrs too late the
inmates are loose

1. *itookcanadianfictionsaysastudentwholovesmunroandfindleybut
   insteadofwritingessayswehadtobringleavesgrassphotosdiaries
   drawingspoemsanythingtoshowourconnexionwiththeearth2/3
   oftheclassgotAhedidn'tigivehimkleenex*

2. *phdoralexamsmilingmiddleclassmiddleagedwomansendless550
   pagesonhowpatriarchyhastotallysilencedherasawoman/writer/
   academic/mothercomfortablywoundedshescroppedherhairput
   silverringsthruoneearnokleenexneededforher*

3. *heterosexualstudentinqueertheoryclasstoolatetodropittheorizing
   AIDSthelocalgay/lesbiansceneaLesBiGayculturalstudiesreader
   everyemilydickinsonpoemanallegoryformaleoppressionand
   seethingsexualitygynofictionswomen(w)ritingfromthebodydoris
   dayaslesbianiconmorekleenexhaveibeenwrongabouteverything
   allmylifesheasksmenokleenex*

im going early ive nothing to contribute cant change all this the
tempest as postcolonial allegory creative canonicity poetics of per-
formance art hypertext and marginality the erotics of de/con-
struction ill be a postfeminist in postpatriarchy pinned on a grad-
students door subvert the dominant paradigm pinned on a woman

professors door ok im going early with the kleenex box singing
cole porter the world has gone mad today and goods bad today and
blacks white today and days night today and anything goes and im
going (tho i grieve for the students) and i leave behind these pod-
people in the bright rubble of the subject theyve pulled down smil-
ing and self-obsessed like very young children in playpens tossing
their toys around waiting eagerly for attention and food kleenex

IN HAWTHORNDEN CASTLE

It matters
that we hear them, the old voices.
Without them we are lost. They wait
for our quietnesses, never desert us.
They are utterly faithful.

There are some
who follow them into photographs –
sepia, black and white, faded to sadness.
Some search libraries for history or poems.
Some hear them in music, hearts pulled
nearly out of them by harmonies of longing.
Others sit in graveyards, questioning
ancestors, family, the gentle dead.
Wherever, they matter. They tell us
who we are, what we might expect.

Here the old voices insist.
They speak from stones, from cool rooms,
hide curled away in corners, whisper down
chimneys, breathe from carved wood chests.
They tease us, catch us unawares.

Only special places speak like this,
have such designs on us.
These voices are older than we know,
grown deep and rich down long generations.
Listen. Listen. The strange syllables
swirl and flow, heap into us, push the pulse,
make us carriers of time.

How we will need them in the thin times.
How we must store them up.

We know,
without being told,
they are shaping us into future.

Scotland 1993

RABBIT

A wheel has gone square
over its body, leaving
it pressed into the road
flat as a cartoon.
But the head is intact,
not squashed at all,
its proper rabbit shape,
and the mouth gapes open
in a terrible snarl,
strange and terrible,
as if it would bite
back, shear clean through
my leg bone, tear
out my throat.
I go on, stupidly
looking behind me,
tense enough to start
running for my life.

UNCONSECRATED GROUND
(A story from 1913)

There on the local beach at Whitley Bay,
A place he loved before it all went wrong,
His old shotgun blew his head away.

And for his son, just fifteen on that day,
A life believing the world was tilted wrong
As to the local beach at Whitley Bay

They took him, made him look, and he heard them say
Things which all his life locked up his tongue.
His old shotgun blew his head away,

And they asked his son just what it was could weigh
So heavy, and why his mother took so long
To get to the local beach at Whitley Bay.

They moved the body, led the boy away.
In a room they put him with the corpse. So young,
And his father's shotgun had blown his head away.

She came at last. They buried him next day,
The grave apart, no healing prayers or song,
For suicide was sin, and at Whitley Bay
His old shotgun blew all their lives away.

RONDELS FOR ELIZABETH, AGE THREE

I.

No birthday can come again
But you don't know or care,
Nor should you, lovely there
At three. Such fuss, and then

More treats, and some magic pen
Spells out that your day is fair.
No birthday can come again,
But you don't know or care,

Your darker thoughts forgotten,
For who or what would dare
Bring worry or a tear

To you? Things start and don't end.
No birthday can come again,
And you don't know. Or care.

2.

You blow the candles out
Then stand there wondering
At the applause. Your wandering
Eyes cloud with sudden doubt,

Puzzled that your cake without
Its brightness is a good thing.
Now you've blown the candles out
You stand there wondering,

But the incipient pout
Soon turns to chattering,
Shining gifts for opening.

We know time wins. It's a rout.
But you, you blow candles out,
And we watch you, wondering.

BY THE MISSISSIPPI
(in memoriam A.L.)

Deep in a summer's humid evening,
From the great slow river they start to rise
Until they fill the hot air with heavy
Drifting curtains, like smoke. They call them fish-flies,

The locals, resigned to this, and they don't like them,
Though at other times the river is a friend,
A muddy familiar giving them a purpose.
They watch the flies drift in, clouds without end,

Rippling nets of them, not noisy, heading
For shore to plaster themselves, weighty and slow,
Stupid, on the first land they can find,
And soon the little town is covered, though

The people take it calmly, closing windows,
Sealing what they can. The season's plague
Is on them from the depths. Is it just here
Or does this happen downstream too? Some vague

Unease must make them wonder as swarms keep landing,
Form deep carpets on street and roof and window.
They stir and shift. They don't do anything
But desperately come to be there, as if they know

It's all or nothing, they can't go back. Slow cars
Crunch through them, sliding when they brake,
Wipers furious. Those walking cover faces,
Take tiny steps, as if on new ice, make

Squishing sounds, shake their feet, and head for home.
A transformation! A blanket over the town!
Distant thunder rumbles from the west.
The light is strange in the cloud come up then down.

Morning, machines will sweep the streets, townsfolk
Tend to houses. Dried and small, the dead
Will soon be gone. A few hours for cleaning up,
Then only talk is left, the shake of a head.

For them it's over. It's not like trying to cope
With the other things that sometimes rise inside us,
Drift through the parted doors of our dark dreams,
Arrive unbidden from some terrible place.

Ours are heavier, wait beneath the surface,
And we're never used to them, poised, threatening
To fly, for they'd rise to cover us, once loosed,
Endless, silent, unstoppable, smothering.

Dubuque, Iowa

STANDING BY STONES

1. Chapel Allerton, Somerset, England

You, my wife, brought to tears trying to read
The leaning stones, wiping the moss off them,
Face to face at last with all these people –

Your great-great-grandfather, his parents,
And theirs. They would have guessed someone would come,
Someone from over there, one day, some Comer

Child or grandchild, for a visit, to see.
Well over a century. You try to copy
Inscriptions, have me take, in the gloom, photos

For Uncle Joe in Iowa and his kids
And theirs. You said we had to come this year,
So we turned off the motorway, through water-meadows,

Along muddy rutted lanes to this little place.
All your life you've known its name, his story.
And I couldn't see them at all, but you just walked

Straight from the churchyard gate up to the stones,
Up to your family, as if you knew
Where they were. As if they had been calling.

2. Somerset to Iowa (1877)

He left here with his savings in gold coins.
All he had. He would have written, months
Later, back to these folk under stones,
That he'd bought land over in America.
Farley, Iowa. Good land. I bet he bragged.

And you, my wife, have one of those gold coins,
A half-sovereign. From Somerset. From Comers.
You smile at me in Chapel Allerton,
Your face wet, part of a family packed together
In an ancient, dark and tumbledown graveyard.
Now you come from somewhere real, somewhere
You can talk about, describe. You say you want
Our children to stand just here so they will know
How small it is, this place, how far a line
Can stretch and hold.

                        This is, come war, come weather,
Come anything our sullen world can do,
Their inheritance, all carved and dated. It
Will pull them here. Insistent in my head
Hardy beats and sings – 'During Wind and Rain'.

3. Farley, Iowa

The farm is gone. The Comer farm is gone.
Your mother's brother, Uncle Joe, has sold it.
He's old now and his kids don't want to farm,
Have different lives in towns. He has coins, too,
From Somerset. His grandfather's. We sit for the last
Time in the farm kitchen, driven for days
To get here before he finally moves out,
Summer lightning starting, the way it does,
The evening air heavy, full of growth.
Joe will move. There's sadness in us all.
And you, my wife, drinking all of this in,
Talking about our children, asking Joe
About the Iowa you left, the people,
The whole big thing that was your life, your childhood.
You used to bike here, on the gravel roads,
From Cascade, for lemonade and ice cream, to see
The barns, the animals. Back in the fifties.
He got to here from Somerset, that man.
Joe talks about the richness of the soil,
Blizzards, tornadoes, heat beyond belief,
Guesses about ships and wagons, breaking the land,
Clearing stones from grass. His grandfather.
What will you do without the farm, you ask him.
I'll be fine, he says. Live somewhere else.

4. *Cascade, Iowa (1992)*

Standing in the graveyard. You, my wife,
Above the little town where you grew up.
Standing among the stones. A quiet hillside.
Here your parents. You've never seen their graves –
Had to leave straight after the funerals.

Flowers burst here. Open sky. Sweet air.
You read their names, then quickly look away.
Ambrose Leytem. Marie Leytem (née Comer).
Another Comer grave. Another stone.
I think of Hardy's family at Stinsford.

We drove here past the house where you grew up.
Slowly. Slowly. Stopped and looked. How long
Since that day I met your parents there,
Those evenings on the patio with drinks,
Watching fireflies. Certainty and peace

On the edge of town, and from half a mile away,
Over the fields, the sound of Dutzy's pedal
Steel, as he rehearsed some country blues,
Filling without strain our long contentment.
Everyone who drove by waved at us.

From up here you look down on your early life.
A sweet wind pours. This openness so different
From the crowded, walled-in Somerset churchyard.
I see you trying to make connections now,
Taking stock, pondering these stones,

Your family. You hug your mother's brother
By her grave. I step back. Our line is strong.
A young man went to find a different place,
So here, because of that, you grieve in the sun.
And Dutzy's gone, Joe says. All your old friends.

5. *Deadwood, South Dakota*

Driving back, we go through South Dakota.
I want to go to Deadwood. Always have.

Buses bring tourists up to Mount Moriah.
More graves up here than houses in the town

And it's still in use. You, my wife. You take
A photograph of me by the famous stones

Of Calamity and Bill. I pose and smile,
Remembering the movies and the myths,

Think of sending prints to English friends.
But I'm sad. Above all I am sad.

6. Cascade, Iowa (1962)

And one night, I recall, before a storm,
The air heavy as air can be, bullfrogs
Chortling in the pond, we sat together
On the warm stones behind your old white house,
(Gone now, like the Comer farm. Gone. Gone.)
Young and happy, our life ahead, hearing
Slow, sweet, over and over, on and on,
Dutzy's guitar sobbing across the fields
'I Forgot to Remember to Forget'.

CROSSING THE SALT FLATS
(for Jean)

The water shallows, becomes its own white bed.
The signs say Reno and California
As the road pulls us from the city and the trees.

Never a place like this, even in dreams.
Never this colour. Bright nothingness, sterile white,
Salt. Just salt, waiting. Nothing moves
Except us and others on the raised highway
Across. We've read about wagon tracks near here
Still fresh after a hundred and fifty years.
And we see where cars have gone through the crust of it,
Veering off the road. Accidents? Dares?
It could swallow you, we guess, dry-mouthed.
Some bare brown mountains way off to the left,
Just stone and scrub. Ahead another ridge
Wearing a dizzy shimmer is Nevada,
Never getting nearer as it should.
Surely this is a dress rehearsal for hell?
No shade. No bird. No grass. No flower. No tree.
Just flat whiteness and a press of heat, telling
Us we're out of place and just hanging
On. There must be life, perhaps in holes,
We say. But can't see where or what. It's close
To the end of the century. And more than that.

Yet other cars seem normal, those inside them
Less frantic than us, less appalled. Or are they
Just stunned behind their dark glasses? Dazed?
Hours go by. Nevada's bare mountains
Finally creep towards us, then a town,
And a diner, with photographs of green British
Racing cars from the 1930s, machines
Which somehow got to this outpost and broke
Records on salt bigger than all England.
Back, far back, the city and its temple.
We have crossed a desert and now drink tea.

Impossible here to think that days ahead,
Through huge monstrous valleys of rock and sand,
The threatening sun behind and over us,
Wait the familiar places we once set out from.
Great hills of pine! Long misty falls of water!
Fields of snow, endlessly cold and shining!
How greedily we will scoop it, digging down
With frozen hands, push it desperately
Into our mouths.

I've been reading Plato, she said.
The willow's fretful curtains
Held us in a private shade.

We felt a long slow heat.
How right, I thought. Plato.
The word so cool, remote.

And I watched her quietly
Watching the calm green water
Slide past us, endlessly.

Silent and deep her eyes.
This tableau, then. We two,
Together inside the tree's

Cave, safe from the world of sun.
But for one long stunned moment
Our shadows outside. There! There!

1959

The servants meet them. They were sent ahead
To open up the house, stock up, prepare
For the family. They know the Count will check
The cellar, then go to look at the boathouse,
While tight-lipped, severe, the Countess will inspect
The kitchen and the entertaining rooms.
It has always been so. He will note the termites,
Rotting wood, and she see fading curtains.
The children will explore the paths to the edge
Of the forest, go to the lake, and run silly
Through the orchard pretending to be lost.

All around, great houses breathe again.
Shutters are opened, cobwebs and dead insects
Brushed away, pine-sweet air rinses the rooms
With their paintings and brocade. The land revives.
But summer comes more slowly every year,
It seems, and these pleasures they have waited for
In the city, in the Russia of too many.
Already the Count is in his white suit, checking
His guns. Cushions are brought out for his chaise,
The wicker chairs on the terrace, the rowing boats.
Invitations stand on the mantelpiece.

They settle in. They're comfortable here.
The new century is talk round the dinner
Tables. There's gossip. The groom leads out horses
For the morning canter. The ladies look for shade.
So it has always been. Shots from hunting
Parties in the woods. Lotions for insects.
Outside all day, the children are turning wild –
Brown-skinned, mature, but still polite at meals.
Cigars and cognac in the summerhouse.
Gruff talk. The ladies move to a sitting-room
For wine, in their embroidered floor-length dresses.

Three months is all they have. In this country
Such days are far too few. Somehow the painting
And the patching up are left again. The termites.
The charcoal-burners haven't called this year.
The children say they want to stay for ever
And cry to think of going back. The flies
Grow heavy and slow. They light a fire after dinner
To keep away the chill. So it was, you think,
And wonder if they ever had time to look,
These people, at the shivers on the lake, or wonder
If the howling they heard at night was coming closer.

My thanks to the editors of the following, where versions of many of these poems first appeared: *Black Apple, Blue Buffalo, CBC Radio, CKUA Radio, Dandelion, Grain, Insights* (Harcourt Brace), *Journal of Educational Thought, The Literary Review of Canada, Nexus, Poetry Nottingham, Quarry, The Road Home* (Reidmore Books), *SansCrit, Seam,* and *Writing Towards the Year 2000* (Beach Holme).

I would like to express my gratitude to the Leighton Studios at the Banff Centre and to Mrs. Drue Heinz for my Fellowship at Hawthornden Castle. Special thanks to John Metcalf; to Myrna Sentes and Michael Bradford for help with preparing the manuscript; above all, to my wife, who, as always and in so many ways, has made the writing of these poems possible.

Christopher Wiseman was born and educated in Britain, and after some years writing and teaching at the University of Iowa and the University of Strathclyde in Glasgow, he came to Canada in 1969. Since then, he has taught at the University of Calgary, where he founded the Creative Writing programme. His poetry, short fiction and critical writings have been published and broadcast extensively in Canada, Britain and the United States, and he makes annual reading tours in the U.K. as well as reading frequently in Canada. Christopher Wiseman's poetry has won two Province of Alberta Poetry Awards, the Poetry Prize from the Writers' Guild of Alberta, and an Alberta Achievement Award for Excellence in the literary arts. He has served on the Board of the Alberta Foundation for the Arts, as President of the Writers' Guild of Alberta, and as editor and poetry editor of both ARIEL and *Dandelion*. This is his eighth full-length collection of poetry.